PRODIGIOUS KIN

LUCAS MARTEN

Cover art by Magi Purnomo (@magipurnomo)

ISBN Print: 978-1-970260-00-7
ISBN eBook: 978-1-970260-01-4
ISBN Audiobook: 978-1-970260-02-1

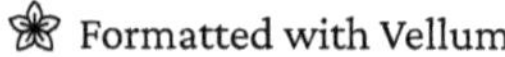
Formatted with Vellum

CONTENTS

YOU

Who are you?

You are someone's child, whoever you are.

You became in an organ and grew your own little body,

it got big until you became the you you are right now.

That's who you are.

You are a part of everything, whenever anyone says anything about

everything,

they're talking about you, and me, too.

. . .

Not all good, not all bad, lots of both.

Kind of like you.

But enough about you, let's talk about "them."

"They" are just like you, too, kind of like me.

They grew up out of stardust, walked out of the oceans,

evolved into primates, primated into you...

They work, they learn, they expire.

They sleep, they wake, and everything in between.

That's the thing about them,

they're basically you,

if you were just a little

Different.

PEACHFUZZ

A tortoise of utmost purpose and highly detrimental ethics. Adopted, lost, abandoned, free. This tortoise begins on a destructive journey of self-loathing and later becomes one with the universe.

While on the path to enlightenment, Peachfuzz strikes up conversation with a rather attractive narwhal whose proportions are quite offensive by modern standards. A century on, an unforgettable narwhal in the heat of summer, lacking the boundaries of a typical reptile. While enjoying an unnatural amount of horn and scarring, the tortoise becomes aware of cognition's limits on romantic endeavors. Can one love what one cannot understand? Can one be loved by something so lovely? How to grasp the complexities of interspecies communication is a puzzle even the politest of tortoises must grapple with at some point in their miserably long life.

While one mark of reptilian goodness can be assuaged into a minor inconvenience, a lack of chaotic greed among a sea-dweller can be interpreted as unforgivable weakness. An oceanic creature cannot abide the limits of land-dwelling dimensions. A connection that lacks the promise of ups and downs but replaces them with forwards and backwards is without a failure indeed.

And so the tortoise walks on, despite the as-yet untouched tribulations of modern relationships, foreseeing better things ahead and moves into yonderous nothings without a moment's ponder. On the way to glorious nothing, Peachfuzz discovers the delights of sand and light, the crisp green of an adult seedling, the warmth of the closest star, the cool that comes with a large rock in the distance, to go on despite the earth and the wind that try to push you into retreat. There is no adequate shell from all of nature's harsh beauties, but nor is the unprotected life worthwhile without its occasional tremendous falls.

WHAT TICKLES YOUR FANCY

My children, my parents, my family,

to what do we owe this matriarch?

Everything.

Everything, I say.

Do you know what it is

to scrimp?

You don't. You can't. You haven't and you will not.

You haven't scrimped because she has scrumpt.

She gave us a home, all and each and every one of us.

Through a Great Depression or two, through pandemics of the air and soul, there has always been Eleanor's.

Eleonor walks the halls of Eleonor's even now.

She stays in a place with a thousand rooms,

Whispering to the produce and straightening the bedsheets.

She turns off the screens,

There's one on every wall,

floor tile, and shelf divider.

She wipes her eyes, a lone tear tracing the scar

that got her into this business in the first place.

It's her childhood dream, aglisten asunder, amountain of mundane and good:

a new stock option, just like the Trumps.

Eleanor flies east to the dining rooms and prepares a midnight snack:

a bluefin, cold, smoked in sesame. Wild arugula and a sprig of dill.

A generous sauce on the side, a little of the good stuff, and a chateau biblánde.

Lastly, a creaméd spinach,

plucked and wet not but four hours hence.

Her favorite.

Truly, to sell food is to love it.

To add a service station, electronics department,

winery, beddery, and a deli,

That's talent.

She cooks, she cleans,

She ramps up the profit margin by five and a half percent

without influencing the congressional district

any further.

Whole aisles of concentrations, maps to betterment, and
every kind of fibrous tissue,

"College Going Away" specials,

the bestselling novels of 1776,

the finest guns o' war ever produced in the U.S. of A.

edible patriots for the Fourth of July.

It's Elvis! Dressed in his infamous garb,

"Good Lord!" aglisten with dewy sweat,

"My hunny's gone bananas,"

he says like he says,

beside the plantains.

Life's what you make it,

So let's make it

30% off for being a frequent customer.

Eleonor's opens at eight,

Ricky's opens at ten (lazy), Barbara's opens at five (unprofitable),

Leanne's will never open again (welcome to the family).

Let it be said that Eleonor was generous,

She rid the world of the storefronts, the bastards,

the seize-holders who grabbed the planet and gave it a bad shake.

Eleonor hugged each and every customer, at least once in her life,

all while dealing with a prescription opiate addiction

(which we will never speak of again).

Turn now to Eric, the shareholder-turned-billionaire whose mother passed this weekend.

Self-Made Eric will hug you from now on,

He will whisper to the produce and straighten the bedsheets, if with a little less gusto,

only because he is the lesser of the two, the past and the future.

he may be a disappointment, with his receding hairline and weak jaw,

and not one scar to tell of,

but it is us who must give to him, if he is ever to succeed.

he needs us now, more than ever.

Eric asks us, begs us, not once to ever hate again.

To love yer neighbor, do nae take the laird's name in vain,

Repeat thereafter your love of Eleonor's,

Not that it becometh of Eric, but because it belonged to Her,

That woman of the ages, who passed not but one week hence.

She never lived a day of her life

reminding anyone of anything

but the day before.

Bless you, customer,

For remaining loyal.

For stimulating the business.

Despite a change in management.

It’s Eleonor’s, baby,
Get comfortable.

BAD NEPHEW

Never wanted to say this about a kid,
You know,
One I watched grow
from a lump of fat on my sister
into a crying shitting thing,
Didn't get much better.

Call this, what, twenty-two years?
Go ahead, okay, yeah, say it,
I don't have any kids.
I don't know what it's like to raise kids.
Sure, point taken, granted.
Granted!

But I'm gonna speak up real quick for pinching your children.

I was regularly beaten as a child, sent to bed without supper,

deprived of water, smacked in the face at a Denny's,

humiliated at a basketball game, destroyed in front of the kitchen sink.

I turned out fine!

You know what I don't get are these all freakin snowflakes.

Where did they come from?

The Navy?

That's an Army joke my dad used to tell.

He said the Navy was where, you know, the guys who were, you know, not as, manly, or...

That's where they would go.

I never served,

I'm kinda hoping my dumbo nephew joins up.

This kid could never fly a plane.

Give him a gun he'd probably shoot himself by accident.

I'm kidding,

Seriously.

. . .

I wanna know his IQ.

I'll bet he's certifiably dumb.

A freakin' moron wacko.

Shoot, put the kid down.

Comes to Thanksgiving dinner in a baseball cap.

Takes his weed walk before the meal and thinks we won't know.

Now he's got Molly involved and look,

Perfect niece, ruined by a bad nephew.

Sorry.

SON JEREMY

Excuse me.
But.

How does one,
approach the world with confidence?
Like, how would you
, for instance ,
Handle a stressful situation?
Let's say the environment was set to sustain you, but then
it became hostile
and you didn't know
why. So you try solving the problem, and you go to school
but then you owe money to the government and the banks
and you're like
what?
Why is this worse?

So you go to a doctor and talk and get touched
but then you're in more debt and can't afford
the meds

and you’re like
what,
what did I do more wrong? You know? Like, what?
What?

What would you do for that, relative?

YOUR SECOND COUSIN AT 80

I’ve been waiting since Tuesday in my favorite armchair next to a fireplace,

suffering,

Spending time like a Dodger, eating microwave meals like some kind of

fucking

type of

dicklicker spitfuck.

That’s it.

Somebody give me their keys.

Dark blue? Fuck you.

I got mad again

Damn it.

Fuck.

The wind through my hair, the smell of salt in the air.

Dang.

Yes,

Feeling good on a Tuesday.

Whoops, a lamppost.

Ohh, *this* guy again.

Tellin me about some kinda vertebrate-scum-o-the-whatsit,

Fuck off.

Eat a dick, Dr.

My body, my voice, you shut the fuck up.

No beer in over a year

and you're

Telling *me*

To "Live healthy"? No,

I don't think so. I don't think so

one damn bit.

Ate my vegetables n shit.

Good at card games,

Pretty good with my hands.

Can tell when a guy's lyin to me.

Got a couple fuckin' kids.

Shit.

Now I've lived

to see the day

MTV sucks.

Fuck.

I'm healthy, I'm the one who's healthy,

Prove to me *you're* healthy, ser.

Show me your vax card, Dr.

Put a mask on when you speak to me, Dr.

Hark, here comes that tetanus shot again, yeah, yeah,

today's the day, Dr., give it to me.

Psych, blam blam, I'm the genius and you're on the floor.

The wind through my hair, the smell of salt in the air,

Outside time at noon.

GATITO

Keepy boy bondaleek.

Schmeakingly wonderful,

wunderbar, gracias.

Oooo so gooky, pleasantly squib, unceasingly present.

Supremely lethargic,

Graciously gracias, bodacious squeak, necessary pip.

Oblivious and wondrous, screeping backway, forwardwise grip.

Katinka, thank you for the times.

They were all necessary.

STOP CALLING

Sanitation called, they want their dirty, disgusting, smelly, gurgling trash can back.

The 2000s called, they want their two cool, not sleep-deprived twenty-somethings back.

My parents called, they wanted a grandchild but probably should have said so before moving to a retirement community a thousand miles away and leaving us without a babysitter.

CPS called, they want an ETA on my wife's EKG, A.S.A.P.

My middle school piano teacher called, she wants to know why I've squandered my musical potential on a sperm-fetus under an as-yet-unproven assumption that playing Bach and Stravinsky to minors makes them smart.

My wife's gynecologist called, he wants to know if I'm honoring the no-sex-for-six-weeks contract that we entered into (without my consent).

My grandfather's doctor called, she says Pop-Pop's losing his vision and should move into our "guest room." You know, because I'm just swimming in guest space and extra food. You know me, *I* have disposable income for an extra adult and their ASL-certified "helping assistant."

That strange number with the same first six digits and an ever-changing last four called, again; they want to know if I'm happy with my internet service provider and if I'd like to switch my car insurance and get a bank loan and take a survey on local issues and go on an all-expenses-paid trip abroad.

The credit card company called, they want to know how I'm doing, if I need anything, anything at all, and they're offering to waive my outstanding fees ("what with the new baby and all") because I'm a loyal, responsible, dependable customer.

Just kidding.

A FRESH BROTHER

We're all "looking forward" to your arrival,

little bro,

but let's get one thing straight:

I won't be giving in to you.

I don't care that you're small, I don't care how big you get. I won't change your diapers.

No stupid movies, no stupid music, no stupid sounds *at all.*

I won't be your role model, I won't let you win at games.

You can't eat my french fries, I'm not going to cook for you.

I won't teach you to drive, I wouldn't give you a job if I could.

I'm not going to tell my friends about you,

I won't tolerate you dating outside your league.

. . .

Now, here's what you can do: You *can* play Nintendo,

you *can* wear my old clothes, when I'm done with them.

You can eat when I eat, like what I like, and go where I go (sometimes).

You will be allowed to live

and I promise not to kill you on purpose

(except in self defense).

So welcome to the family, don't die.

THE ALBATROSS

Grease spinner, dictatorial dragon, Uncle Al. The Ol' Uncle Al, short for Albert, short for Albatross. Haha hoho, at it again.

Dictionary wiz, mastermind genius of brunch next Sunday. Pees with the door open, doesn't mind it at all. Getting old, a northwards Millennial, or a youngerly Baby Boomer who didn't boom out many (any) babies.

Puts his shoes on and does up the loops, ties his shoes like he knows how to. When he takes them off, he leaves them there and doesn't come back for three days. Then he puts them on and takes them away then puts them back and doesn't return for six more days.

Yes he smokes. Of course he smokes. He's got a pack on him right now and he doesn't mind sharing or even giving you your first cigarette on his front porch with a Red Gatorade to wash it down.

He watches the major channels: NBC, CNN, MSNBC, ESPN, FOX, and CSPAN, for laughs. He's up on it, he's into it, wanna talk about it? He can.

. . .

But don't ask him about the president. God damn it, he's got ideas. He's got ideas and maybe even a plan and holy shit you don't want to sign up. You're gonna end up at the bottom of a lake. Who knows how. Maybe the police'll shoot you, maybe you'll shoot yourself, maybe it was Uncle Al, or the butler, or the big ol' D.T. himself. He talks too much, just let him talk until someone comes to rescue you.

Life is short. Pee with the door open. Smoke a cig. Leave your shoes where they are. Move in with Uncle Al and Aunt Alex and find yourself a nice girl. Get a place in the city, close to where she works, make a life and grow up to be a newscaster, just for jokes,

then go back to Uncle Al and say,

"Hey, did you see me on Tuesday?"

TRICKLE

Let the rain come and purify my soul,

O Lorde Colonel Mark Mary Sanders Jr. Beta Sequence Todd.

Open my heart to your joy and wisdom.

Todd me up and wife my material,

Pay my taxes and unify our bank accounts,

Child of God, I pray.

Uno, dos, día tres.

This is the third day without your warm embrace,

chicken fried steak and beta cross super-sequence.

For you, I could Function+commandcommandcommand.

. . .

Our union is more than a keystroke,

it's https-GodMarkSeven.

TIRE CREAM

A Letter of Divorce (Please Don't Respond),

Do you ever watch a piece of dust floating for a long time? That's how I feel every time I use Mendelssohn tire cream. It's not work anymore, it's everything to me. Keeping my tires sparklingly smooth is what keeps me going.

I don't think anything is worth a million dollars. You said that a thing is only worth what people think it's worth. I don't think anything is worth a million dollars except, maybe, Mendelssohn's tire cream. I feel like when I use Mendelssohn's tire cream, it's the only time that I'm really me.

I was meant to be a father. I know that, now that I've felt what it is to care for something. To cradle an axle like a babe, to change oil like a steaming diaper, then drive that sucker to the zoo and absolutely lose it.

I took us to a zenith once, you remember, an after-hours mountaintop, and turned out the headlights. We binged outdoors and I saw the back of your head. We stayed inside and fell asleep to movies. But it's okay, you were still the best thing to happen to the world. I told you that and you believed me.

The first time you started making papier måché flamingóes is when I knew I had gotten you too many tropical fish. Staring and gawking, gluing and perceiving.

And now, sometimes, I look at a piece of dust as it falls from on high. It makes me think of you and our Mendelfish. Fully lubricated tires and a tropical aquarium lit up neon blue and humming humming humming. Your mother on our couch. My fatherhood in a waiting room.

No Bruce Willi-Zeta Jone flick ever lit me up like flushing your goldfish and rubbing my Subaru's tires.

THANKS

Thank you, [name and/or relationship], yet again, for the generous gift of [thing].

However, this being the time it is, I feel I must ask for more. While your gift of [thing] is appreciated, money is what I truly need. I've seen movies, where family members will give each other a lot of money, maybe like a loan where they have to pay it back. Or, you know, not pay it back.

While ten or twenty dollars is nice, I have to ask if we could... multiply that by a thousand? If you can. If you can't, I understand. But because I'm young and history kinda says that money has to, I don't know, flow downwards, then it's, like, a good thing to give money to a younger person. Especially one who needs it. Especially ones you're related to. So I'm writing to you, today, to please send money. ASAP.

. . .

With love,

Me

Your response:

____

____

____

Banking Information Line One: ____________________

Banking Information Line Two: ____________________

Amount: ___,___,___.00

Government Signature: _______________

With love,

____

[You]

COOLEST SISTER EXITS ASYLUM

It's a story, now. It's the tale of a drive to Sommersville,

A hand out the window with a cigarette and my longest draperies.

Loaded with chakras and balanced by

balance boards,

Adorning the porch like four scores of pork.

She's the most hectic spectacle.
I've never seen her like.
Within and without, I believe her to be,
fully and completely,
okay enough.

Three tablespoons of ground meats,

A mixed-in mixing-spoon with flavor,

And a tiny toothpick with a flag on top.

And a **sparkler**

It's called Measly Maybel's Feasibly Tasty Deliciously Crazy Whacked-up Wednesday

Meatball Mess of a T-Ball's Best Sunday, Smith, of a Nother Time Some Meatball.

It's not a mess, **you're** a mess,
Telling me to imbibe, locking the door and letting me out again,
Freedom to eat, freedom to sing, freedom to rub my hands and say
"I'm having a meatball memory."

I wrote the most rancid poem, doctor.

Doctor?

BARRY BONDSMAN

I screamed from ten feet away,

"I think it's going to rain on Friday,"

but they couldn't hear me.

"You're always whispering,"

she says.

I've never **WHISPERED** in my goddamn **life**.

Do I LOOK like the kind of guy who *whispers*?

She tells me, listen to this,

that sometimes, I do whisper.

Okay?

Fine, I heard it.

But I don't whisper.

Do I SEEM like the kind of guy who gives a **shit**
That you didn't hear me?
I don't *ASSUME* that no one is listening to me,
I know they're there.
I know exactly who it is
that's there.
And I don't whisper.

I've been outside plenty.
I've been in public often.
I go to events, sometimes.

People like me are my people.
We sit at tables and talk. And not in frickin' *whispers*,
We're **loud** boys, the loudest everywhere we go.
You can hear us if you want to,
I don't give a shit.

I grew from a seed of a thing to a thing of a thing,
A big fuckin' legal adult.

I'll have a house someday

And I **guarantee** it'll be bigger than *yours.*

CHAMELEON JACKSON

Chameleon Jackson,

18/80.

Good score for the boy, been climbing up a storm.

Thought I'd never see a reptile at 16 getting higher than me on a Saturday aha

Boy, things have changed since you and me first came acquainted.

You but a little thing and so were I,

Slurping GoGurt and snacking on crickets,

Both drinking water.

Love you, baby.

Through breakups, nightmares, and one allergic reaction,
through a lightbulb outage and nasty cricketses,
you have grown into a jack of all trades, an entrepreneur
and a scholar.

I fucking love you, my boy.
Every time you look at me, especially with both eyes,
I know you see me as I really am:
Just a man, in love, with you.

And so I say to you with all my heart,
Happy Birthday,
Enjoy the Waxworms.

FREAK

Not many people know this, but I live right by the iguana factory.

You might not know this about me, but I'm liable to see an iguana

or seven, walking down the street, all singing the same tune.

I'm cognizant, I'm conscious of what I'm saying and what I've seen.

You don't know iguana as vermin, but I do.

There is no freedom whilst in the presence of an iguana, that's what they do.

That's what vermin do. We hate them, they hate us.

Our life is a war and death is release.

. . .

I don't mind a factory, nonetheless.

The air is fine, if you don't mind a cough.

The water's good, if you don't mind the taste.

And the products are solid, if you don't mind cheap shit that sucks and is shit.

It's not about what the factory makes, it's what the place *produces.*

Vermin. Stupid. Freaks.

Don't work

Don't pay

Only take.

Looks

Bad.

Step on it, scuttles.

Spit at it, it might... I don't know.

Damn it, you know what I say.

Death IS release.

You don't know it until you've seen it, coming for you both.

Me and you, the enemy and the friend, the self, the self as friend.

The enemy's friend's sexual partner, laying eggs on my porch.

. . .

Squelch squish splat.

JIGGLY SQUIBBLE, THE INGRATE

Why isn't Jiggly Squibble pibbling yet?

As a mere teenager, I started making hashtags with plant-based materials and selling them at industry-level markup per international regulatory standards.

Why can't Jiggly do the same?

I'm fiscally responsible as a trend-setting homemaker,

retired before my first colonoscopy.

Why is Jiggly still freeloading and freebasing like a regular doodlespit with a deathwish and a tractor-trailer?

I don't sell my children for spoons or my spouse for forks,

I make a living doing needlework and designing logos for underprivileged children.

I'm a father.

I'm a saint.

. . .

Jiggly just jiggles and eats leftovers from a trash heap

without so much as squeeging a peen.

I've seen it with my own eyes, I see it every minute of every night

Online.

It's not that I'm mad at a person,

it's that I'm outraged at a group

and experiencing no other problems in my personal life.

Lock away the scrunge and give them menial and degrading tasks.

Give them uniforms and boxes to check,

telling us about the times they wasted on "fun" and "games."

It's the working world, dick-ass,

Wake with the sun and sleep with the moon.

Sell your body and eat Karl's Jr.

I'm going to start suing,

not in an angry way.

Just to get Jiggly off the couch and contributing to society,

Not because I'm mad,

but because I'm good at being

and I think other people should be,

too.

WHAT CAN'T BE SQUEEGED

Some people get by in life with nothing but a squeegee.

Let me tell you, squeeqeeing is not everything.

You can't squeege every thing.

Like this, this is Aversian Craft, you don't run a soapy squeege

over the wood or the plush.

You can't squeeege a marriage together for seventeen years.

You have to do more than squage and say,

" Hey , Look What I Did Today ! "

It's not enough, you dimwit.

It's not enough, you lunatic, Neanderthal.

Try making a meal.

Try changing a diaper.
Try diapering a change, I don't know I'm so tired.
Just *do* **something**.
Just **do** *anything*.

Keep the house. Keep the children.
Keep the tv, you can even keep my dog.
I want my book, I want my peace lily,
and I'm **keeping my** credit card.

I'm going to Fiji.

~

I've been to Fiji.
I have swum with turtles.
I have done a drug.
I surfed the Mamanuca on the limb of a shaved tree.

And yet I never knew peace.
I never felt the embrace of family
in the sands of Tavarua.

. . .

And yet, I liked it.

Being alone.

And so,

as needed,

I will vacation.

A SCREWJACK FINDS

A fuckboy of the lowest degree, the greatest upon greatest of grandsons.

My boy sews his seed, with pride and danger, he dances and he sews,

he sews and he dances. He spreads our legacy and truly truly

fucks.

At times I wonder, with limited potency, what goes through the boy's mind.

As I saw in his father, love and marriage and marriage and love.

And his father before him, a man of much marriage and little love.

But wherefore with this boy? Many little loves

and not one marriage.

. . .

Still I continue, what next of the fucker?

Will the man not slow?

Does the body not give?

I imbue no strength, I give no guidance, I humbly request: Enough.

And yet he continues, with me at his crown,

to give up his all and blend the boundaries.

For a moment, on a mycelium Saturday,

I think he sees me, and considers his place.

He perceives the multitudes, the spectrums outside his understanding and mine.

He meditates on all, and, as usual,

comes up short.

Between the truth of fractals and animal rights,

Dickass sees only himself in the mirror

while I see only his great grandfather.

Two men who played, nothing more.

They existed. They grazed at love and screwed themselves.

They spread darkness and dove into glass,

Then went home.

And here I find my voice again, regretful but fine. My wife, my father, my daughter.

And now this, serpent-dicked spinster.

He may be in a state of constant frenzy,

with the wherewithal of his grandmother,

but still I wonder:

Could the boy not at least wear a condom?

THON DARTH MONAHUE

And then,

upon twisted bent,

Mine self awoken to a splash and sizzle.

But when I put my heart down, and gave it my everything,

a one came upon me and denied denied denied.

It's okay, I'm used to deny, I don't care, I'm well-adjusted.

I'm a nice guy, my wants and needs are few.

So I go forward, with nice guy behaviors and nice guy situations.

I told everyone around me "Hi" and "Hello,"

and yet not one said it back.

Not one wanted to know about my Ajax and twirl.

Not one made me best man nor one of the girls.

Which is fine, it's okay, I'm used to deny deny deny.

So I slumbered onwards.

I awoke in the spring of my discontent, waving and shallowing,

"Hi"

"Hello"

and then I saw her, beautiful and blue,

sallied and struthered.

I, a prince, and she, a shepherd.

She asked me to light her cigarette,

and I left because that's gross.

And so on I alight, me a prince and the world a stage.

Granted I'm fine, nothing matters and I maintain mystique and good credit.

I lift, I wait, and now it's my birthday.

It's my birthday, son, and I congratulate myself, yes yes yes.

Eat of cake and drink of wine, watch of tv and tell the internet who I am.

No I won't change.

No, I won't graciously lose my cool.

And no, I won't be sharing my cake with you any time soon.

I've chosen.

I've selected me. I'm my champion and it's my bad girl summer.

I'm going to flex my muscles and waddle, soon, when the weather's right.

AUNT STEPHANIE

I don't like to make a scene,
or cause a ruckus.
It's best to slowly disintegrate,
over a period of zero to one hundred years.
Sit in the corner,
all the time.
Participate in the conversation,
eat my lunch.

I close the doors I come through,
I leave the toilet seat up,
for the men.

I stanza repeatedly,

when I'm supposed to.

I pray not to die in my sleep.

If I should die before I wake,

Please, no, do not take.

If I should die when I wake,

Please, no, not tomorrow either.

I have a week to get through.

I'm living for others,

I don't think life is a dream.

I believe in reality.

I am. Not. Violent.

I hit a deer with my car and killed it myself with my hands with these hands.

I reach climactic tension when I think I'm supposed to,

but then I tell you about my lemon squares and powdered sugar,

returning you to reality.

Gently.

SISTER VIOLET, CARNIVORE

Violet (somebody's daughter, probably) eats the people herein.

She expunges and re-consumes. Once, twice.

You find yourself digested once, twice. Violet has escaped.

The world is hit with realization.

Each and every one decides,

to love and be loved,

to care for others and protect the planet,

until Violet eats them, too.

Violet tracks all thinking beings in the universe and eats them.

When she finishes her holy meal, she reaches catharsis

into a black hole

and throws herself in as well.

The universe knows peace.

www.ingramcontent.com/pod-product-compliance
Lightning Source LLC
La Vergne TN
LVHW011051110826
845149LV00015B/3456

* 9 7 8 1 9 7 0 2 6 0 0 0 7 *